3. **Martinique.** Paul traveled to this Caribbean island, hoping to find the same kind of beauty he remembered from his childhood in Peru. Paul painted his first tropical scenes in Martinique.

 4. **French Polynesia.** At the age of 42, Paul Gauguin traveled across the world to Tahiti, one of the French Polynesian islands. Paul visited other islands in the area, too. He painted some of his most famous works while living in these beautiful South Sea islands.

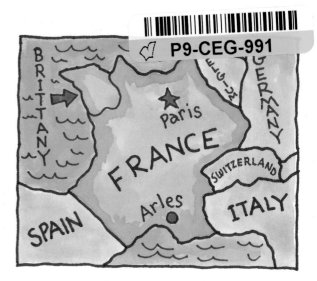

TIMELINE OF PAUL GAUGUIN'S LIFE

1848 Paul Gauguin is born in Paris, France, on June 7.

1851 The Gauguin family leaves France for Lima, Peru. Sadly, Paul's father dies during the voyage.

1855 Mrs. Gauguin returns to France with her family.

1865 Paul leaves school to join the Merchant Marine, a fleet of ships that delivers cargo all over the world.

1868 Paul joins the French Navy and continues to sail all over the world.

1872 Paul begins a job as a stockbroker. He becomes very successful.

1873 Paul meets Mette Gad. They get married the same year.

1874 Paul becomes interested in art. He begins painting as a hobby and visits as many art exhibitions as he can.

1876 Gauguin works hard at becoming a good painter. He enters his work in art shows and collects the work of other artists.

THIS WAY

UP HERE

1879 -1882 Paul Gauguin is invited to exhibit his paintings at yearly Impressionist art shows in Paris.

1883 Paul Gauguin loses his well-paying stockbroker job. He decides to become a full-time artist.

1886 Paul travels to Brittany for the first time. He will visit this ancient historical region of France often to paint the people and villages there.

1887 Paul travels to the Caribbean island of Martinique.

1888 Paul spends time in Arles, France, as a guest of Vincent van Gogh, who attempts to set up an artist's colony there.

1891 Paul travels to Tahiti. Except for a short trip back to France, Paul spends most of the rest of his life in Tahiti and other South Pacific islands.

1901 -1903 Paul Gauguin spends the last years of his life on an island called Hiva Oa. He dies there on May 8, 1903.

GETTING TO KNOW THE WORLD'S GREATEST ARTISTS

P A U L
GAUGUIN

WRITTEN AND ILLUSTRATED BY MIKE VENEZIA

CONSULTANT MEG MOSS

CHILDREN'S PRESS®

An Imprint of Scholastic Inc.

To Mike Weiler—media tech advisor,
dog trainer, son-in-law, and friend

Cover: *Matamoe (Peacocks in the country).* 1892. Oil on canvas,
115 x 86 cm. Pushkin Museum of Fine Arts, Moscow, Russia/
Erich Lessing/Art Resource, NY

Library of Congress Cataloging-in-Publication Data

Venezia, Mike, author.
  Paul Gauguin / by Mike Venezia. — Revised Edition.
    pages cm. — (Getting to know the world's greatest
artists)
  Includes bibliographical references and index.
  ISBN 978-0-531-21666-8 (library binding : alk. paper)—
ISBN 978-0-531-22105-1 (pbk. : alk. paper)
  1. Gauguin, Paul, 1848-1903—Juvenile literature. 2.
Painters—France—Biography—Juvenile literature. I. Title.
  ND553.G27V46 2016
  759.4—dc23
  [B]   2015035326

1 2 3 4 5 6 7 8 9 10 R 25 24 23 22 21 20 19 18 17 16

Self-Portrait with Hat. 1893. Oil on canvas,
18 ^{1}/$_{10}$ x 14 ^{9}/$_{10}$ inches. Musée d'Orsay, Paris. Art Resource, NY

Paul Gauguin was born in Paris, France, in 1848. He led an adventurous life, traveling all over the world to find just the right place to paint.

Old Women at Arles. 1888. Oil on canvas, 28 $^7/_{10}$ x 36 $^2/_{10}$ inches.
Mr. and Mrs. Lewis Larned Coburn Memorial Collection, 1934.391.

Paul Gauguin often used flat,
bright colors and simple outlined
shapes in his paintings.

Self-Portrait.
1889. Wood,
31¼ x 20¼ inches.
Chester Dale
Collection.
National
Gallery of Art,
Washington, D.C.

Sometimes he would use symbols
from the Bible, like the snake, the
halo, and the apples in the painting
above. The symbols he used gave a
look of mystery to his paintings.

Paul Gauguin is probably best known for his paintings of life on the faraway islands of the South Pacific. He loved the colors he found in the jungles, the native people who lived there, and their ancient customs.

Day of the God. 1894. Oil on canvas, 26 8/10 x 36 inches.
Helen Birch Bartlett Memorial Collection, 1926. 198.
Photograph © 1991, The Art Institute of Chicago. All rights reserved.

7

When Paul was very little, his
parents decided to move from Paris,
France, to Peru, a country in South
America where Paul's mother had
relatives.

Paul saw things there that he
would never forget. Strange and
beautiful plants, flowers, monkeys,
and jungle birds were all over the
place.

When Paul Gauguin was a teenager, he got to see other faraway parts of the world, too. First, he got a job on a cargo ship. Later, he joined the French navy. While he was a sailor, Paul learned how to box and how to duel with swords.

Paul's many travels and adventures may have helped give him the imagination he would later use when he became an artist.

Paul didn't decide to become an artist until he was all grown up. He had a family and an important job in Paris. Paul was a stockbroker. He made lots of money by showing people how to invest their savings wisely. Paul started painting as a hobby on Sunday afternoons with a friend he met at work. The picture on the right is one of the first paintings he did.

Landscape. 1873. Oil on canvas, 19 $^9/_{10}$ x 32 $^1/_{10}$ inches.
Fitzwilliam Museum, Cambridge, England.

The Market Gardens of Vaugirard. 1879. Oil on canvas, 26 x 39½ inches.
Purchased 1953. Smith College Museum of Art, Northhampton, Massachusetts.

Many of Paul Gauguin's first
paintings remind people of the work
done by a group of artists known as
the Impressionists.

Interior of the Artist's House. 1881. Oil on canvas, 51 $^3/_{10}$ x 63 $^9/_{10}$.
Photograph by Jacques Lathion, © Nasjonalgalleriet, Oslo, Norway.

Paul liked the soft colors the
Impressionists used and the natural,
everyday scenes they chose to paint.

Paul was able to meet many of the Impressionist artists and other artists who lived in Paris.

He learned important things about painting from them.

Artists such as Edgar Degas, Camille Pissarro, and Vincent van Gogh liked Gauguin's style of painting.

Some of the Impressionists even asked Gauguin to show his work alongside of theirs at an Impressionist exhibit. There were artists, though, including Claude Monet and Paul Cézanne, who didn't think much of Gauguin or his work.

Paul was encouraged by his artist friends. Soon painting became much more than just a hobby for him. It was practically all he could think about, even at work!

Finally, Paul Gauguin decided to quit his job and become a full-time artist. He didn't have much luck selling any of his paintings, though, and soon ran out of money. He moved his family from Paris to Copenhagen, Denmark, where they lived with his wife's family.

Paul's wife, Mette, wasn't happy about his decisions, but she loved Paul and knew how important painting was to him. She went along with his wishes for as long as she could.

Breton Girls Dancing, Pont Aven. 1888. Oil on canvas, 28¾ x 36½ inches.
Collection of Mr. and Mrs. Paul Mellon. National Gallery of Art, Washington, D.C.

Things didn't go well in
Copenhagen, and Paul decided to
return to Paris without Mette.

Paul Gauguin was always in search
of a place to paint where he could
really express his feelings. He soon

The Yellow Haystacks. 1889. Oil on canvas, 28¹⁵⁄₁₆ x 36⅝ inches.
© Photograph R.M.N. Musée d'Orsay, Paris.

became fed up with the busy, uncaring city of Paris. He thought there were too many rules people had to follow, especially rules about art. He found what he was looking for in Brittany, a part of western France.

It was there that Paul Gauguin's art really started to change.

Paul liked the unusual costumes worn by the people of Brittany and the beautiful countryside he found there. Paul started painting with brighter, flatter colors. He not only painted what he saw in Brittany, but added things from his imagination.

Paul's work soon became popular with many artists around Europe. They liked his new decorative style that was filled with expression.

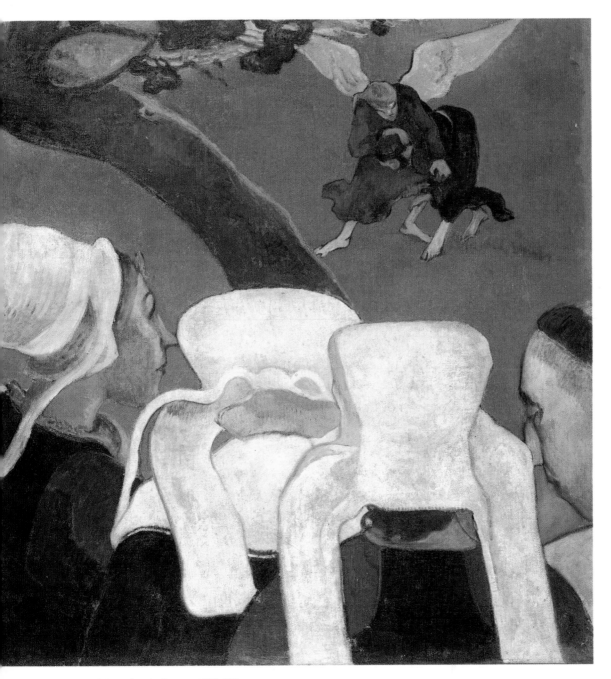

Vision After the Sermon. 1888. Oil on canvas,
28¼ x 36¼ inches. National Gallery of Scotland.

Even though Paul's paintings were well liked by his friends, he still didn't have much luck getting anyone else interested in them. He decided that to make his work better, he would have to leave France.

Paul left for the South Sea island of Tahiti in 1891. He told his wife and children that they would get back together someday. He believed they would, but they never did. Except for a short trip back to Paris, Paul spent the rest of his life in the South Seas.

Paul was a little disappointed when he arrived in Tahiti. It was run by the French government, and part of it reminded him of the place he had just left! Paul soon moved into the wilderness and explored other islands to find what he was looking for.

Tahitian Landscape. 1891. Oil on canvas, 26¾ x 36½ inches.
The Julius C. Eliel Memorial Fund. The Minneapolis Institute of Arts.

Paul worked very hard in Tahiti to put his own special feelings into his artwork.

Unlike the Impressionists, who tried to paint nature as they saw it,

Fatata te Miti. 1892. Oil on canvas, 26¾ x 36 inches.
Chester Dale Collection. National Gallery of Art, Washington, D.C.

Paul Gauguin used his imagination to rearrange nature and create worlds that he dreamed about. He hoped that a person would look at one of his paintings and dream of their own imaginary worlds.

Where Do We Come From? What Are We? Where Are We Going? 1897. Oil on canvas, 54¾ x 147½ inches. Tompkins Collection. Courtesy, Museum of Fine Arts, Boston.

Paul was finally happy with the way his artwork was turning out. He was so excited about the painting above that he worked day and night for a whole month until it was finished.

The people in this painting seem to be wondering about the questions the title asks.

The beautiful colors Gauguin used and the way he made it feel filled with life make this one of his greatest paintings.

Even though Paul Gauguin was happy with his artwork, he led a very unhappy life in the South Sea Islands. He was sick most of the time, and very poor.

Right: *Self-Portrait at Golgotha*. 1896. Oil on canvas, 29 $^9/_{10}$ x 25 $^1/_{10}$ inches. Photograph by Luiz Hossaka. Museu de Arte de São Paulo, Brazil.

Ta Matete. 1892. Tempera on canvas, 28 $^7/_{10}$ x 36 $^2/_{10}$ inches. Kunstmuseum, Basel, Switzerland. Giraudon/Art Resource, NY

To create his own style, Paul often borrowed ideas for his paintings from Japanese prints, stained-glass windows, and Persian and Egyptian art.

He is also known for the wood carvings he made in Tahiti. Many of them have the same feeling the island people gave to their own mysterious carved wooden idols.

Right: *Pere Paillard*. 1902. Wood, 26 $^3/_4$ x 7 $^1/_8$ x 8 $^1/_8$ inches. Chester Dale Collection. National Gallery of Art, Washington, D.C.

Left: *Bonjour Monsieur Gauguin*. 1889. Oil on canvas, 44 $^4/_{10}$ x 36 $^2/_{10}$ inches. National Gallery, Prague, Czechoslovakia. Giraudon/Art Resource, NY

Paul Gauguin painted ideas that came from deep inside his mind. His paintings influence artists to this day.

It's fun to look closely at a real Paul Gauguin painting. You can see he often painted on cloth that was used to make sacks for carrying fruits and vegetables. He used the rough, bumpy surface to give his paintings a special look. The paintings in this book came from the museums listed below.

The Art Institute of Chicago, Chicago, Illinois

Fitzwilliam Museum, Cambridge, England

Kunstmuseum, Basel, Switzerland

The Minneapolis Institute of Arts, Minneapolis, Minnesota

Musée d'Orsay, Paris, France

Museu de Arte de São Paulo, Brazil

Museum of Fine Arts, Boston, Massachusetts

Nasjonalgalleriet, Oslo, Norway

National Gallery, Prague, Czechoslovakia

National Gallery of Art, Washington, D.C.

National Gallery of Scotland, Edinburgh, Scotland

Smith College of Art, Northampton, Massachusetts

Detail of *Ta Matete* on bottom of page 30.

LEARN MORE BY TAKING THE GAUGUIN QUIZ!

(ANSWERS ON THE NEXT PAGE.)

1. Who were three important artists who encouraged Paul Gauguin when he first decided to become a painter?
- a Paul Cézanne, Vincent van Gogh, and Camille Pissarro
- b Michelangelo, Andy Warhol, and Georgia O'Keeffe
- c Norman Rockwell, Frida Kahlo, and Jackson Pollock

2. What instrument did Paul Gauguin enjoy playing?
- a The tuba
- b A Steinway concert piano
- c The guitar

3. The two most famous roommates in the history of art were Paul Gauguin and Vincent van Gogh. Vincent wanted to start an artist's colony in Arles, France, and invited Paul to stay with him. Why did Paul suddenly leave Vincent after a short time?
- a Vincent criticized Gauguin for painting outside the lines.
- b Vincent refused to make Gauguin's favorite dessert—ever.
- c Vincent was always starting arguments that made Gauguin uncomfortable.

4. Paul Gauguin wrote a book about his experience living in Tahiti called *Noa Noa*. In the Tahitian language, what does *Noa Noa* mean?
- a Stop that. You're making a mess.
- b Very fragrant land
- c The porpoise-driven life

5. What were some of Paul Gauguin's favorite tropical island foods?
- a Roasted pig, fish, guava, and poe
- b Soft-serve ice cream, mac & cheese, and BBQ baked beans
- c Lasagna, walnut pesto, and French fries

ANSWERS

1. **a** Gauguin often painted alongside Cézanne, van Gogh, and Pissarro. Early on, he learned a great deal about painting by copying and discussing the styles of these great artists.

2. **c** When Paul Gauguin traveled to Tahiti, he brought his guitar and mandolin along. Paul looked forward to sitting under tropical trees and strumming tunes to attract new friends.

3. **c** Gauguin and van Gogh learned a lot from studying and discussing each other's paintings. Unfortunately, a troubled van Gogh often turned their experience into a series of angry, hotheaded arguments. After only two months, Paul Gauguin decided to leave Vincent.

4. **b** In the Tahitian language *Noa Noa* means "very fragrant land." Gauguin loved the smell of the wonderful island flowers, fruits, and other surprising scents he discovered while living in the islands of the South Pacific.

5. **a** Paul wrote about a meal he had at an island wedding. He enjoyed roasted pig cooked on hot stones, fish of all kinds, and many exotic fruits and veggies. For dessert, Paul was probably served poe. Poe is a favorite Tahitian pudding treat topped with coconut-milk sauce.